An I Can Read Book®

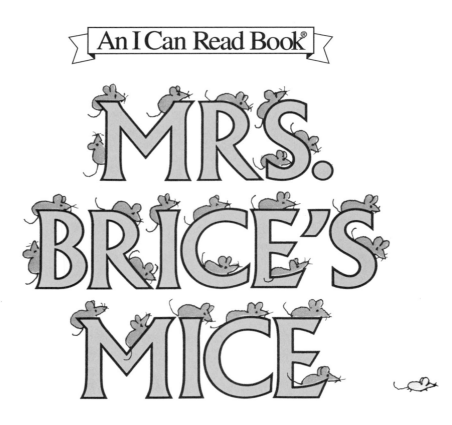

MRS. BRICE'S MICE

Story and Pictures by

Syd Hoff

HarperCollins*Publishers*

HarperCollins®, 📖®, and I Can Read® are trademarks of HarperCollins Publishers Inc.

Printed in the United States of America. For information address
HarperCollins Children's Books, a division of
HarperCollins Publishers, 195 Broadway,
New York, NY 10007.

Library of Congress Cataloging-in-Publication Data
Hoff, Syd, 1912–
    Mrs. Brice's mice.
    (An I can read book)
    Summary: Mrs. Brice has twenty-five mice and they
all do everything together.
    [1. Mice—Fiction]   I. Title.   II. Series.
PZ7.H672Mhi 1988   [E]   87-45680
ISBN 0-06-022451-7
ISBN 0-06-022452-5 (lib. bdg.)
ISBN 0-06-444145-8 (pbk.)

16 17 18 19 20 PC/WOR 40

MICE

For D.B.H.,

the one and only

Mrs. Brice had twenty-five mice.

She fed her mice

the finest cheese.

She washed and dried them
behind their ears,
so they were always clean.

7

Mrs. Brice loved to sing for them.

When she played the piano,

twenty-four little mice

danced around her.

One very small mouse

danced on top of her hand.

He was afraid to fall

between the keys.

When Mrs. Brice went to bed,
twelve little mice
slept on one side of her.
Twelve little mice
slept on the other side.
One very small mouse
slept on the clock,
in case he wanted to know
what time it was.

In the morning,

Mrs. Brice did exercises.

She stretched

her arms and legs.

She bent over

and touched her toes

with her fingers.

12

"One, two, three,
four, five, six....
One, two, three,
four, five, six...."

Twenty-four little mice
did exercises too.

They stretched,

they bent,

14

they touched their toes.

One very small mouse

kept on sleeping.

"It is time for our walk,"
said Mrs. Brice.

Twelve little mice
walked in front of her.

Twelve little mice
walked in back.

One very small mouse
sat on top

of Mrs. Brice's hat,

so he could see

where they were going.

He saw a cat.

Twelve little mice
ran this way.
Twelve little mice
ran that way.

One very small mouse
jumped down to the ground
and ran this way and that.

He ran so many different ways,
the cat got tired of chasing him
and went back
to whatever he had been doing.

"What a clever little mouse
you are," said Mrs. Brice.
"Now we can go
to buy some food."

Twenty-four little mice
sat in a cart
and enjoyed the ride.

One very small mouse
sat in front.

They went up one aisle.

They went down another.

Mrs. Brice bought

food in cans,

food in jars,

cold food,

hot food.

"Now we can go home,"
said Mrs. Brice.
Twenty-four little mice
were glad.
But one very small mouse
kept on leading the way.
He led them
to the dairy counter.

Mrs. Brice bought

a nice, big cheese.

28

Then she and her mice
went home to eat it.

After they ate,

Mrs. Brice sang

and played the piano.

30

Twenty-four mice

danced around her.

One very small mouse

kept right on eating.